LIBRARY
ANDERSON ELEMENTARY SCHOOL

W9-AOC-667

OTHER BOOKS BY HAROLD W. FELTON

LEGENDS OF PAUL BUNYAN

PECOS BILL: TEXAS COWPUNCHER

JOHN HENRY AND HIS HAMMER

FIRE-FIGHTIN' MOSE

BOWLEG BILL: SEAGOING COWPUNCHER

COWBOY JAMBOREE: WESTERN SONGS AND LORE

NEW TALL TALES OF PECOS BILL

MIKE FINK: BEST OF THE KEELBOATMEN

A HORSE NAMED JUSTIN MORGAN

SERGEANT O'KEEFE AND HIS MULE, BALAAM

WILLIAM PHIPS AND THE TREASURE SHIP

PECOS BILL AND THE MUSTANG

JIM BECKWOURTH, NEGRO MOUNTAIN MAN

EDWARD ROSE, NEGRO TRAIL BLAZER

TRUE TALL TALES OF STORMALONG

NAT LOVE, NEGRO COWBOY

BIG MOSE: HERO FIREMAN

MUMBET: THE STORY OF ELIZABETH FREEMAN

JAMES WELDON

JOHNSON

HAROLD W. FELTON
Illustrated by Charles Shaw

DODD, MEAD & COMPANY, NEW YORK

Copyright © 1971 by University of Nebraska Foundation
All rights reserved
No part of this book may be reproduced in any form
without permission in writing from the publisher
Library of Congress Catalog Card Number: 72-132625
Printed in the United States of America

To Stan and Hazel

CONTENTS

1

GENERAL GRANT COMES
TO JACKSONVILLE

"GENERAL GRANT is coming to town," said Jimmy.

"Who is General Grant?" asked Rozy.

It was in 1877. The town was Jacksonville, Florida. Jimmy was James Weldon Johnson. He was six years old. Rozy was John Rosamond Johnson. He was four.

"General Grant won the war. He and President Lincoln," Jimmy explained. Rozy didn't know about the war, but he would learn. Jimmy didn't know too much about it, but every Negro boy in Florida learned something about the Civil War. Every boy, if he searched, could find soldiers' buttons and buckles, and perhaps even a bayonet in the sand beside the river or along the road where soldiers had camped.

The great war between the Northern and Southern states had ended only a dozen years before. It had brought freedom for slaves in the United States. General Grant had commanded the Northern armies and after the war was over had served as President of the United States for eight years. He was a great hero to the black people in the Southern states. Jimmy had heard of General Grant for as long as he could remember.

Mr. and Mrs. Johnson hurried to the railroad station with Jimmy and Rozy running beside them. A big crowd was waiting when the train came to a hissing, groaning halt. The engine puffed softly as General Ulysses S. Grant and his party were greeted by the important people of the town, both white and black.

Later, the parade came. General Grant stood on the veranda of the big hotel. Jimmy's father was the headwaiter in the hotel and Jimmy had often been there. The Negro school children with their teachers were to be in the parade. They lined up to pass in review before the famous general.

They were all proud and happy to be so close and get a good look at the great man who had led the Northern armies. But Jimmy wanted to get closer. He wanted to do something special. He had a plan, but as the time drew near he wondered if he would have the courage to follow it.

The band was playing a brisk tune. The long line of children went up the steps and marched the length of the veranda in front of General Grant and the group of important people with him.

Jimmy's mind was alive with question as his class came close. Should he, or shouldn't he?

The sound of the trombones rose. The cornets seemed to sing out notes of courage. The drums urged him.

Yes, he would do it!

When he passed in front of the guest of honor, Jimmy stepped out of line. He looked up at the general, smiled, and put out his hand.

The famous man looked down and saw the eager brown face, the bright, twinkling, gray-blue eyes, the wide smile, and the open hand of friendship. He reached down and shook Jimmy's hand.

Jimmy stepped back into the line of march. He, James Weldon Johnson, had shaken hands with the great General Grant!

2
JIM'S FAMILY

JIM'S MOTHER and his grandmother told him of his ancestors. The adventure in their lives made him wonder what his own life would be like.

One of his great-grandmothers was born in Haiti and married a French army officer. When Haiti was torn by war, she and her three children were sent to Cuba for safety. But their ship was captured by a British privateer and all on board were taken to Nassau, a small island off the coast of Florida.

Although they had lost everything except the clothes they wore, the family found protection and prospered in Nassau. One of the sons, Stephen Dillet—who was to become Jim's grandfather—was first a tailor, then the postmaster, the chief inspector of police, and a member of the Governor's staff. Jimmy loved to hear about his grandfather. He must have been a great man!

Then there was his other great-grandmother. She came from Africa on a slave ship bound for South America. The War of 1812 was on, and the ship was captured by a British man-of-war and all the slaves were brought to Nassau. The young woman was taken into the home of a sea captain and later married him. Their daughter, Mary, became the wife of Stephen Dillet and was Jim's grandmother. After Stephen Dillet's death, she married John Barton, and they moved to Jacksonville when Jim's parents did.

Jimmy's mother, Helen Louise Dillet, was born in Nassau. She went to New York with her mother as a child and received a good education. His father, James Johnson, came from Richmond, Virginia. He was born a free man, but Jim never knew very much about his father's family or how they got their freedom.

As a young man, James Johnson worked in a hotel in New York City. It was there that he met Helen Louise Dillet. She was singing at a concert, and he immediately fell in love with her.

That was about the time the Civil War had started, however, and Helen Louise's mother feared that the black people living in the North would become slaves if the South won the war.

"We are going back to Nassau," she declared. "I'm going to stay as far away from slavery as I can."

James Johnson was not discouraged. "I'll follow you," he told the young girl he loved.

And he did. He became the headwaiter at the Royal Victoria

Hotel in Nassau and, in 1864, James Johnson and Helen Louise Dillet were married.

After the Civil War ended in the United States, the Johnsons moved to Jacksonville, Florida. It was a shabby house that they first moved into, but they were not the kind of people who got discouraged or gave up easily. James worked hard at the big hotel in Jacksonville and Helen Louise became a teacher at Stanton, the Negro school. Soon they built a new house.

On June 17, 1871, James Weldon Johnson was born. His brother, John Rosamond, arrived two years later. Shortly after, their parents adopted a fifteen-year-old girl, Agnes Marion Edwards.

It was a happy home, and Jim was proud of his family. Who knew what he might do when he grew up?

3

THE SPRING-BOTTOM PANTS

JIMMY JOHNSON did what most other boys did. He went fishing. He flew kites. He played games, marbles, shinny, tops, baseball. Most of all, baseball. He played very well and whenever he could, he read *Sporting Life*, a magazine in which he could learn about the great professional baseball players and their records.

His mother read to him when he was very young. Later, he read every book in the family bookcase. Jimmy liked books.

He had as many scraps with other boys as a lively boy should have and he received his share of spankings. He and Rozy both had chores to do around the house—filling the lamps with oil, cleaning the chimneys, trimming wicks, helping wash and dry the dishes, raking the yard, polishing the steel table knives by pushing them up and down in sand.

He went to school at Stanton, the only Negro school in town. And he did some things that all boys did not learn to do. His father spoke Spanish and he taught his sons to speak it too. His mother played the piano and taught Jim and Rosamond to play. Rozy could play better than Jimmy, but Jim tried hard to keep up with his younger brother.

Rosamond did not play the guitar as well as Jim did, though. His father instructed him and he could play it very well before he was big enough to hold it on his knee. His method was to stand it on the floor and play it like a bass viol player handles his instrument.

Grandmother Mary Barton operated a small bakery business in her house. Jim often helped her and they became very close to each other. When he was thirteen years old, he went to New York with his grandmother to visit his great-aunt Sarah. It was an exciting trip, filled with steamboats and trains, ferries across the East River between New York and Brooklyn, visits to Lord and Taylor's big store on Grand Street.

The next year, his mother, Agnes Marion, and Rosamond went to New York for a visit. While they were gone Jim stayed with his grandmother.

Mary Barton was a very religious woman and under her influence Jimmy went to church almost all day Sunday and several times during the week. The preacher wore spring-bottom pants, wider at the bottom than the bell-bottomed pants sailors wore. They took Jim's fancy.

"I want a pair of pants like the preacher's got," he said, watching his grandmother carefully. He didn't know what she would think.

"The preacher wears them," said Grandmother Barton. "I guess it would be all right for you to have a pair too, only—"

"Only, what?" Jim asked, fearful that she might change her mind.

"There's the money. I wonder how much they are."

"Fourteen dollars," said Jimmy quickly. He had already been to the store to find out the price.

"Fourteen dollars!" Mary Barton cried. The way she spoke made Jimmy think it was almost a million dollars.

"I could earn it," he said.

"I guess you ought to," said Mary. "If you are big enough to think you can wear long pants, and spring-bottom pants, at that, you ought to be big enough to earn the money to pay for them."

Jimmy had been working Saturdays at the neighborhood store, earning fifty cents a week. He got a pencil and began to figure. Suddenly he looked up at his grandmother. "Why, it will take me twenty-eight weeks to earn the money," he said. "I can't wait that long!"

His grandmother smiled.

"I'll get a better job," he declared.

The next day he went looking for work and found it, carrying bricks on a construction job. The pay was two dollars a

week and the work was much harder than at the grocery. But it would take only seven weeks to earn the money for those pants.

Soon he was promoted to driving a horse and cart. The pay was then three dollars a week. The spring-bottom pants were almost his.

Soon they *were* his. He was awfully proud of those wonderful spring-bottom pants.

All summer he had practiced on the piano. He had found a new piece, one that Rosamond was sure not to know. He decided he would learn to play it so well that he wouldn't make a single mistake. Rosamond would be jealous of him when he heard him. He certainly had some surprises for his family when they would be all together again.

When his mother, Agnes, and Rozy returned from New York, Jim and his grandmother and father were at the station. Jim was wearing his spring-bottom pants.

When his mother saw her son in his new trousers, she laughed. So did Agnes Marion, and Rosamond laughed the loudest of all. But Jim was undismayed. He liked his new pants.

When they got in the house, he grinned as he went to the piano. Rosamond would be surprised. He played his new piece without a mistake.

Rosamond was impressed, but he too had a surprise. He played the latest waltz tune, straight from New York, and he played it with real ability. Jim sadly admitted that Rosamond was a far better piano player.

That wasn't the worst part. Rosamond had seen General Grant's funeral. Jim had always been someone special because he had shaken hands with General Grant. But no more. Rosamond had seen his funeral, a very fine funeral, with twelve black horses, each led by a black man, and there was a big band too, and a long procession.

Well, he would just keep trying. There must be some way to get the best of a younger brother. At least Jim had spring-bottom pants.

4

PITCHER FOR
THE ROMAN CITIES

Jim Johnson was the pitcher for a baseball club called The Domestics. The catcher's name was Sam Grant. All of the players were Negro boys, fourteen to sixteen years old.

At that time one of the best Negro professional teams in New York was the Cuban Giants. During the winter many of the players worked in St. Augustine and Jacksonville hotels. They played ball in towns in the area to entertain the guests.

One of the Cuban Giants took an interest in Jim and showed him some of the secrets of pitching. Jim soon learned to throw curve balls. He had an excellent "inshoot," a wide "outcurve," a "drop" and a "rise." In addition, he had good control and a fine fast ball.

There was an adult Negro team in town called The Roman Cities. They had won over all the other local teams in neighboring towns, and a game was arranged with a winning team from Savannah, Georgia. Jim's special ability with a baseball was well known and The Roman Cities asked him to pitch for them. Sam Grant was to catch.

"You just come and we'll put you in Roman Cities' uniforms," said Bill Broad. Bill was the best batter Jim had ever seen and a remarkable outfielder. But all the red and blue suits of the men's team were too big for the two boys to wear.

"Gee, I can't wear this suit," said Jim. "It's so big I feel like I'm lost in it."

"I can't wear one either," said Sam. "It's way too big for me."

"We've got to go and get the white suits we wear when we play with The Domestics," said Jim.

The Roman Cities was a top-grade ball club and very popular. It was the champion team of all the towns near Jacksonville. The Savannah nine had a long string of victories back of it too. The game promised to be a good one. All the sports fans in town, white and black, turned out.

The throng streamed in until the ball park was packed. Jim Johnson felt a shiver of excitement and wondered for a moment if he could play in the company of grown men?

He looked around at the crowd. His eyes ran down the bench, looking over the men he was to play with. He knew that he and Sam would not do well at bat. But then he thought about the pitches he could throw and what a good catcher Sam was. Confidence flowed through him. All he had to do was to go out there and play ball—and that he could do.

When the Savannah pitcher was warming up, Jim got a chance to see the style of the man he was going to pitch against. The opposing pitcher had a remarkable windup and delivery. He had a fast ball, a very fast ball, and delivered it with perfect control.

"Look at the speed ball," Jim said to Sam. "I never saw a ball go that fast before."

"Don't let that worry you," said Sam. "The Roman Cities picked you to pitch. They must think you can do the job."

Once he stood on the pitcher's mound, Jim dismissed any troubled thoughts. Sam was right. The Roman Cities had selected him for the job. If they thought he could do it, he would!

"Pitch it to me," Sam Grant urged as he crouched behind the plate.

Jim heard the chatter of encouragement from the infield. He heard foghorn words of comfort coming from Bill Broad in center field.

For a starter, he laid a wide sweeping curve ball squarely over the plate. The batter pulled back.

"Strike one!" the umpire cried.

The game was on. Jim struck out one after the other. He had decided the kind of game he would play. He would change pace. He would keep the other team off balance, keep them guessing.

The innings wore on. He used his inshoot, his outcurve. The

speeding ball seemed aimed at the batter, then it suddenly turned
to pass directly over the plate. When the batters thought they
had learned the ways of the strange ball, Jim switched, and the
ball seemed to be going far wide of the plate, only to turn and
pass over its center.

Each inning brought its own challenge. When a batter found
the ball, there were some fine players back of the pitcher. Then
there was Sam behind the plate. His team was with him. The
crowd was with him.

Something exciting was going on, something Jacksonville
ball fans did not often get a chance to see. They left the side-
lines and crowded behind the wire backstop so they could see
the ball curve and drop and rise. Each wild swing of a batter
brought cheers and whoops of joy.

Jim won the game with sixteen strike-outs and a lop-sided
score in favor of The Roman Cities. He was proud and happy
as people from Jacksonville roared their pleasure.

Before the cheering died down a crowd gathered around him.
"How do you make a ball act up that way?" someone asked.

"It's a trick of some kind!" another exclaimed.

The man who had pitched against Jim moved into the crowd.
"What I say is that he must put something on the ball that
makes it look like it's making all those curves," he said. "Maybe
a man can throw a curve ball all right. But not such wide
curves. It's not possible!" Though he had lost the game, he was
a good pitcher and his opinion was respected.

The manager of the Savannah team interrupted. "If that's so, what happened?" he asked. "The boy struck out sixteen men. Some of my best batters too. And he's only a kid," he added with wonder in his voice.

"Look here, Johnson," the big pitcher said. "No foolin'. Does that ball really move around like it seems to?"

"Show 'em, Jim," Bill Broad said. "I've seen you do it lots of times."

"Sure. Show 'em," Sam Grant urged.

The crowd followed Jim as he walked toward two trees that were about a dozen feet apart. He stopped about fifty feet from them so that the trees were almost directly in line with him.

He wound up. The ball left his hand. It passed to the right side of the first tree, then it curved, and passed the second tree on its left side.

The demonstration of his curve ball caused almost as much excitement as the game.

"Well, I'll be!" said the pitcher from Savannah.

"I still can't believe it!" the manager declared.

5

JIM CROW

When he was a small boy, Jimmy Johnson had a prompt answer for people who asked him what he wanted to be when he grew up.

"I'm going to be the governor of Florida," he would say.

That ambition faded when his attention centered on the horses and mules that pulled the big dray wagons with their heavy loads through the streets of the town. They were huge animals, and the men who held the reins became his heroes. He wanted to be a drayman.

That lasted until he saw the drum player in the Union Cornet Band. Martin Dixon could roll a drum without stopping longer than anyone else anywhere, Jimmy was sure. That's what he wanted to do. There was nothing like a drummer!

Then for a time he wanted to be a soldier, to go to West Point. Only a few Negroes had done that, but some had made it. After his success with The Roman Cities, he thought of playing professional baseball, though no black man had ever played with the big league teams.

When he started to work at a regular job, it was on a newspaper route. The pay was $2.50 a week and he gave Rosamond fifty cents to help him. He worked for the *Times-Union*, and before long he became an office boy. Sometimes he was allowed to hold copy for the proofreaders. By the time he was sixteen and finishing school at Stanton, he had been promoted to an assistant in the mailing room. He considered becoming a newspaperman as a career.

He knew he couldn't do that, or much of anything worthwhile, without a good education. But if he was to go on to high school and college he would have to go to another city. Stanton had only eight grades. There was no high school for Negroes in Jacksonville.

The Johnsons had both white and black neighbors and friends. Jim had never had any unusual problems about race or color, but he was beginning to think that being colored was a problem in itself. People said that all opportunities were not open to Negroes, and it seemed to be true.

His mother said it was not so. "A black person can do anything a white person can do," she said. "Study hard. Learn. Get an education. It may be harder for a Negro, but you can do anything you set your mind to do."

"I can't go to high school here in this town," said Jim. "I can't sit downstairs in a theater."

"Maybe not. Not now and not here anyway. But that is wrong, and wrong cannot last forever. You just go ahead and do your part. Do the best you can. Things will come out all right."

There were a number of Negro schools to consider—Hampton Institute, Howard University, Fisk, Biddle, Atlanta University. Family discussions were long as the advantages of one or the other were talked over. Rosamond was thinking about school too. He wanted to study music, and dreamed of going to the New England Conservatory of Music in Boston some day.

There was a new member in the Johnson household who was also interested in schooling. Ricardo Rodriguez was a Cuban boy of about Jim's age who came to live with the Johnsons for several years. He had been sent to the United States to learn English and get an education. Jim and Rosamond were delighted to have him. They knew a limited amount of Spanish from their father. Now they had a marvelous opportunity to really master the language. They learned as much or more Spanish from Ricardo as he learned English from them.

Finally it was decided that Jim would go to Atlanta University. It would mean hard work and sacrifices, but it was a fine school, with preparatory classes for students of high school age. It was closer to Jacksonville than the other colleges, and the train connections were good. Still, it was almost 300 miles away and Mrs. Johnson was happy that Ricardo would also go there to prepare for the study of dentistry.

The two boys made their preparations for the trip. When the

day arrived, they were too excited to eat. Among their luggage was a lunch packed for them by Jim's mother.

They had first-class tickets and so got aboard the first-class car of the train. Jim and Ricardo leaned out the window and waved happily to family and friends on the platform as the train pulled out of the station. They did not notice that the other colored people who got on the train had gone into another car, nor did they notice that they were the only two black people in their car.

The conductor came. Jim pulled the tickets from his pocket and handed them to the man. "You boys got to go in the car up ahead," he said.

"Isn't this the first-class car?" Jim asked.

"Yes, but you can't stay here."

"But we have first-class tickets."

"No matter. You've got to go in the colored people's car," the conductor replied.

"If we have the tickets, why can't we ride here?"

"It's against the law, that's why!"

People in the nearby seats were listening to the conversation. It was Jim's first experience with a Jim Crow law, one just recently passed in Florida, segregating the races in railway cars.

Ricardo was not able to understand what was going on. The English words were spoken too fast for him. *"Que dice?"* he asked Jim in Spanish. "What is he saying?"

Jim replied to Ricardo in Spanish. The conductor listened,

unable to understand what they said. The foreign language impressed him. He stood there uneasily while the two boys talked
in Spanish. Finally he moved on and said no more about them
moving.

The boys stayed in the car. On his way to school, that very
first day, Jim learned something. Dark-skinned people from
foreign lands who spoke another language were treated better
than black Americans.

6

NEW DIRECTIONS

JIM AND RICARDO took examinations to determine how far they had progressed in school, and then were assigned to classes. Ricardo was a special student because of his lack of command of English, but he made rapid progress with it.

Jim soon found that Atlanta University was quite different from Stanton. A great deal more was expected of students. It took long, hard hours of study to keep up, and still more to excel. He found that he was able to handle mathematics. His knowledge of Spanish made Latin quite easy, as was French. Some other subjects were more demanding.

He enjoyed a manual training course in woodworking. The smell of freshly cut wood, the feel of a newly polished surface, the handling of tools gave him real pleasure.

Every student was required to work for the school for at least an hour a day. Carrying wood to the kitchen stoves, or hauling ashes away, cleaning, working on the grounds or in the kitchen—there were hundreds of tasks that needed doing. There were also many pretty girls always ready with admiring looks and smiles. At mealtimes the girls sat on one side of the tables and boys on the other. Both Jim and Ricardo were considered special because they could speak Spanish. Jim attracted attention too because he could play the guitar and he had been to New York.

There were two hours of freedom from study and work during the day. Sunday school, church, and prayer meeting took up most of Sunday, but Saturday afternoon was free. There was usually baseball, and always visiting and talking. Jim was pitcher for the baseball team, and sang with the school quartette.

He took time to explore the library's shelves. He had always loved books, and now he began to write poetry. Thoughts that came to him were jotted down in notebooks, and often those thoughts were expressed in rhymes and verses.

Just meeting other students was stimulating. At Atlanta there was constant talk and exchange of ideas, especially about racial discrimination and the place of the Negro in America. It was clear that there was a long, hard fight for equality, but Jim saw that the Negroes were not entirely alone. Many of the teachers at the University were white, and because they ate their meals with black students, the white teachers were not welcome in the homes of most white families in Atlanta.

Most of the students at Atlanta were from the best educated and most progressive and prosperous black families in the country. But not all. For the first time Jim met students from the backwoods areas. He was shocked to find out that they knew nothing of things he had learned at home and took for granted— of regular habits of bathing and cleanliness, of keeping up a good appearance. Some had never even seen a stairway before.

While Jim was interested in developing his ability to write, he had another goal. It was one he had thought about ever since he had failed so miserably as a small boy when he tried to speak a piece at Sunday school. He wanted to learn public speaking. He felt a bit sheepish when he confided this to Ricardo.

"I'm going to learn one thing before I leave this school," he said. "I'm going to learn to speak in public."

"But you do," exclaimed Ricardo. "You do that every day. I'm the one who has to learn to speak, not you."

"You'll do all right. Your English is getting better every day. But my tongue gets all tied up when I get up in front of people. I want to be able to get up and speak my ideas, clearly, so they will understand."

And Jim did. He joined the debating club. A prize at the end of his first year gave him a real feeling of accomplishment.

When vacation time came, Jim and Ricardo returned to Jacksonville. It was good to see the family again. Rosamond had grown. He had made great progress in his piano playing and had developed a good singing voice.

Jim's pitching arm was in good shape and he expected a happy summer of baseball, swimming, and good times. But his mother became seriously ill with rheumatism. Four months in bed would

leave her crippled for the rest of her life. His father, now a minister at a church in Fernandina, a small town about thirty miles from Jacksonville, was distressed.

A yellow fever epidemic broke out. The fever sent Jim to bed, and while he soon recovered, his illness and his mother's condition made it clear that he could not return to school that fall.

He resolved to continue his studies as best he could. First, a job was necessary, and he got one as a timekeeper for a road gang. The pay was two dollars a day. Then, his father found a tutor for him, a Jamaican who was a cobbler but a brilliant scholar.

One day, early in the winter, a friend told him that Dr. T. O. Summers needed someone to take care of his office. Jim applied for the position.

"What schooling have you had?" the doctor, a young white man, asked.

"I finished at Stanton, and I have studied for a year at Atlanta University," Jim said.

"Indeed? What did you study there?" Dr. Summers asked.

"English, history, algebra, Latin—"

"Latin?"

"Yes, sir."

"Here. Let me hear you read Latin." The doctor handed him a small volume he took from a bookcase.

After he had read a few sentences, Dr. Summers said, "Thank you. I think you will do."

The job was to receive patients and take care of the reception room, but Jim was soon acting as clerk, bookkeeper, and bill collector.

He and Dr. Summers became good friends. Jim discovered that the doctor wrote poetry. He was eager to read what Jim had written and to offer advice. The doctor's excellent library provided an introduction to classic literature, and Jim became more aware of the art of writing. Poetry came to occupy a more important place in his life.

Dr. Summers had made a close study of the yellow fever epidemic and he was asked to come to Washington to make a report on his findings. He invited Jim to go with him.

It was an eye-opening trip. Jim knew that Ricardo and Rosamond were envious of his good fortune. He and Dr. Summers went by way of New York where Jim visited his aunt briefly. In the nation's capital he saw the White House and the Washington Monument, and listened to debates in the Senate and House of Representatives. The close contact with Dr. Summers influenced him too. "You'd make a good surgeon," the doctor told Jim, "but you are also a poet."

At home in Jacksonville, Jim looked back over the year he had thought would be a lost one. He had been unhappy at the thought of missing a year of school. It was odd the way things worked out. He had gained friendship, encouragement, inspiration, and kept up his studies. He was a wiser and better young man.

7

THE PROFESSOR

THE NEXT YEAR, Jim finished two years of study in one year. By studying during tne summer he completed his high school work and was allowed to take the college entrance examinations in the fall. He passed them and became a University freshman.

Money for room and board was always necessary, but Jim Johnson was never one who liked to be idle. He turned his woodworking course to good use, and earned money operating a lathe. He also had a job in the University printing office. But he still found time for baseball, and for palling around with the fellows. He played the guitar and sang bass in the University quartet that traveled through New England one summer, singing songs and performing skits, and collecting money for the good work Atlanta University was doing.

During the first summer after his freshman year Jim taught school in a back-country Negro farming district in Georgia.

Children there could go to school for only two to four months in the summer during the slack season, after the crops were "laid by," and before the harvest.

He boarded with a poor farm family with a school-age son named Lem. His room was separated from the rest of the house by a flimsy wall papered with old newspapers. There was no running water, no glass in the windows. He bathed in an old washtub that was brought to his room. The rest of the family washed themselves on the porch of the cooking shed outside. The two lamps had only broken chimneys and Jim seldom had one to himself for reading in the evenings. But he continued his habit of writing, using spare minutes before darkness came to add essays and poems to the notebooks he always carried with him.

Still, the place was clean, and the eagerness of Lem to please him and to learn made up for a lot.

"Do you really think I can learn to read?" the boy asked. "Out of a real book?"

"Sure you can," assured Jim. Lem was about fourteen years old, but with his enthusiasm and some encouragement Jim was sure he would master a beginner's reader.

Jim's pay as a teacher was five cents for each student each week. The school was an old, rough board, unpainted one-room building that was the local church. When he started his classes he had two dozen pupils. Before the summer was over the small room was packed with fifty children, all eager to learn.

School was from eight in the morning to three-thirty in the afternoon. One day a group of solemn looking men came to see the teacher. They were very serious, and dressed in clean but ragged, patched clothes.

Jim waited for one of them to speak.

"We're the school committee," one said. He was a tall, lean man with grizzled white hair.

"What can I do for you?" asked Jim.

"Well, Professor"—Professor was what all the students and their parents called Jim—"we sees you got school open from eight in the mornin' 'til middle of the afternoon."

"Yes. That's right."

"We figgers you ought to keep open longer."

"Most of us never had no schoolin' but we want our younguns to learn. We work from sunup to sundown. Seems like they oughta do it too."

"But that would be a long time," said Jim. "I think the children might get tired sitting on these hard benches so long."

"I gets tired workin' too," the man insisted.

"But sitting and studying are different. They will learn better if they don't have to sit in one place on these hard seats so long."

"You think so?"

"I'm sure of it. You know yourselves. When you sit on these benches during church, they get to seem pretty hard, don't they?"

"They sure do," the man quickly agreed. "I don't like church to last mor'n 'bout two, three hours."

By this time the men were beginning to fidget. The seats were indeed uncomfortable. The thought of sitting there for seven hours was not a pleasant thought. The committee solemnly rose, quite happy to be free of the hard benches.

"You can help the children learn as much as possible by seeing that they do their homework at night," said Jim.

"We do that all right, Professor," the white-haired man said as they left the building.

Jim walked the two miles to school and back each day, and on Saturdays he hiked seven miles to the little town of Hampton to get his mail and to visit with a friend and fellow student who was teaching there. He also had a chance to get a more varied meal from his friend's landlady. The first two weeks with Lem's family he was served chicken every day. Then the chickens were gone, and there was only fat pork, greens, corn bread and buttermilk, day after day.

Jim found Lem to be a pleasant boy, anxious to learn. It was a shame that he would have so little schooling. Jim gave him all the help he could.

The tall, thin boy told Jim many things about animals, crops, the weather, birds, and plants as they walked to and from school. Jim was sure he learned almost as much from Lem as Lem did from the Professor.

Lem was very interested in Jim's toothbrush. He watched every morning as Jim used it and finally said one day, "That's sure some brush you got there. What's it for?"

"To keep my teeth clean," said Jim.

"I ain't never seen one of those. I just use this," said Lem. He ground the end of a twig between his strong, white teeth until it was frayed at the end. Then he rubbed his teeth with it.

"But what's that white stuff? I never had none of that." There was a great wistfulness and yearning in the words.

"Here. Try some toothpaste," said Jim generously.

Lem beamed and seemed delighted with the taste. Jim thought he had never seen anyone quite as happy. He made up his mind that next Saturday when he went to town he would bring back a toothbrush and toothpaste for Lem.

A few days later when Jim went to brush his teeth after breakfast, he found Lem had borrowed some of his toothpaste. And that was not all. Instead of using his homemade twig brush, he was using Jim's toothbrush.

"Jest a minute, Professor, an' I'll be through," said Lem happily.

Jim began to wonder how long Lem might have been using it. He stopped himself. That could not be changed now, and Lem had no notion that he had done anything wrong. He knew nothing about sanitation or hygiene.

"Tell you what, Lem. You just keep the toothbrush," Jim said.

"Professor! You mean it? Honest?" Lem was overwhelmed with gratitude.

"And the paste too," said Jim.

Jim had never seen people as poor or with as little opportunity as the black people he met that summer. They were tied down by ignorance and poverty. The few white people in the neighborhood took no interest in them and their school. Poverty and the helplessness and hopelessness it produces became Jim's enemies. Surely there was some way to help these people.

He was filled with wonder that the black people there could live and laugh under such conditions. But they did laugh, and Jim sometimes thought that the fact that they were able to laugh was what made it possible for them to continue to live as they did.

8

STANTON GETS A NEW PRINCIPAL

JIM WAS GRADUATED from Atlanta University in 1894. He could have had a scholarship at Harvard in medicine, but he chose to accept the post of principal at Stanton, his old school in Jacksonville.

He headed home, wondering what it would be like. His father was still preaching. His mother had given up teaching since her illness, but his sister Agnes was a teacher at Stanton. Rosamond had gone to Boston to the New England Conservatory of Music. Ricardo was also in Boston studying dentistry. Other friends had scattered. Would he find it dull at home?

At Stanton there were a thousand students and twenty-five teachers. The classes were large and the teachers spent long hours at their work. The youngsters wanted to learn. That was one reason why Jim had undertaken the task of principal. Ever since his teaching days in rural Georgia, he had felt the immense importance of an education.

His lessons in the little one-room schoolhouse had given him no experience in the management of a large school like Stanton. He decided it would be a good idea to see how the white schools were run. So, with the consent of the superintendent of schools and the white principal, he visited a white school to observe their classes and procedures. That visit had a result that was quite unexpected. There were complaints by some white parents, who heard about it from their children. What was a Negro doing visiting a white school?

The school board held a special meeting. The white superintendent and the principal of the school Jim had visited were as shocked at the clamor as Jim was. The three men attended the meeting and told the school board it was silly to complain just because a Negro principal had visited a white school to study the teaching methods there. The school board agreed, and the matter was dropped.

There had been a race riot in Jacksonville. There was something different about the atmosphere now. Relations between whites and blacks were more tense than before. There were rumors and suspicion, friction and distrust.

Jim came to know Mr. Gilbert who ran the bicycle repair shop. He would drop into the shop for parts for his bike and to talk with Mr. Gilbert, whom he liked. Mr. Gilbert was a white man, and they often discussed the difficulties and injustices that black people faced.

One day in the bicycle shop there were several white men. The subject of race came up and Jim spoke freely, far too freely for a Negro to speak at that time in the South. He spoke of the hurt and the suffering of black people, of the unfairness of Jim Crow laws, of prejudice.

The discussion was lively and brisk, but there had been no anger shown. Suddenly a young fellow with crude manners broke in. "What wouldn't you give to be white like me?" he shouted at Jim.

If Jim was stunned at the bad taste of such a question, some of the other men seemed to be amused. A few of them chuckled. Mr. Gilbert was not pleased. He was as hurt as Jim.

There was a long pause. Most black people in Florida would have changed the subject or retreated in silence. Jim stood his ground. He pushed aside the anger that was rising within him. He looked at the man.

"No. I would not like to be white," he said. "Most certainly I would not want to be like you. In such a change I would be the loser. I much prefer to be what I am."

He didn't know what might happen. In the South, Negroes did not speak in such a fashion to white people, especially not in Jacksonville at this time.

Finally, one of the men said, "Well, Tom, you asked a question, and you got an answer. Satisfied?"

"Yes," said one of the others. "That was a stupid question. None of us got to choose what color we are anyway." He

nodded to Jim. "Well, I've got to be goin'. So long."

The men filed out of the shop. Some of them gave Jim a smile. One or two muttered a word of apology.

Such things made Jim wonder how he could overcome a serious problem in his school. Twenty-six children were to be graduated at the close of his first year as principal. There should have been well over a hundred, but many had dropped out before they reached the eighth grade. Jim wanted the twenty-six to have a chance to go on with their education, but there was still no high school for Negroes in town. Any black child who wanted to attend high school would have to go away, as Jim had done. Most of them did not have the money to do that.

He was sure that if he asked the school board to start high school classes for Negroes, he would be refused. What could he do? How could he help his new graduates?

At last he thought of an answer. He would have a freshman high school class without telling anyone except the students and their parents. He would teach the class himself.

He found a quick welcome for his idea in the people he spoke to. In the fall, the class assembled and he taught them the same courses he had at Atlanta in his first preparatory year. It was most successful.

If he were to have both a freshman and a sophomore class the next year he would need help. He went to Mr. Glenn, the superintendent.

"I probably should have told you before now," he said, "but

I have been teaching a high school freshman class at Stanton."

Mr. Glenn looked puzzled.

Jim continued. "That's right. Now they have finished the year and they want to go on to a sophomore class. And I'd like to have a new freshman class."

"You taught the class yourself?"

"Yes. And at no expense to the taxpayers." He smiled with Mr. Glenn.

"And with no objection from the school board," Mr. Glenn added.

Jim laughed. "That's right. They didn't know about it. But now I'm afraid I won't have time to teach both classes. I'd like to have an assistant."

"Why, I think that can be arranged," Mr. Glenn replied. "I'll get you an assistant. If white people protest, we'll just have another session with the school board like we had last year."

"And we'll surely come out on top again too," said Jim.

"Indeed we will. Your children at Stanton ought to be entitled to the same kind of education as all the other children in town. You've done well, Jim. I'll find you an assistant somehow," Mr. Glenn declared.

Each year a new class was added and a new teacher assigned to help Jim. In four years, with the cooperation of the superintendent, Jim had made Stanton a high school.

9

THE BAR EXAMINATION

J IM WAS TROUBLED by incidents such as the one in the bicycle shop and others he had experienced. What was wrong? Black people should be allowed to enjoy all the rights other people had. Yet everywhere he looked he saw abuses and inequality. He wanted to do something about it.

Teaching, being a principal—that was good. But perhaps he could reach more people if he were to write. He had once wanted to be a newspaperman. Then he could put words into print. He could point to the wrongs.

Was that enough? Merely to write and put down on paper the facts and arguments? Was there another way? What about becoming a lawyer? He could bring cases to court so that the law could correct the wrongs.

He was on his way home and reached the sidewalk leading to his home. He put his bike in the shed and walked across the porch and into the house. This would take some more thinking. One man couldn't do it all. But one man, in his own small way, could help.

Jim and a few friends started a newspaper for Negroes. He used several hundred dollars he had saved and borrowed more from his father. The other papers had columns of news of special interest to black people, but Jim wanted to present the arguments for equality for Negroes—in schools, public transportation, business opportunities, and all other areas.

The paper was called *The Daily American*. It was the first Negro daily newspaper in the United States. Jim was the editor, and wrote both editorials and news stories with enthusiasm. The paper was very popular and influential at first, but the promise it held was soon lost, as well as the money invested in it. Within eight months *The Daily American* had to be discontinued. There was just not enough public support.

Jim continued as principal of Stanton school, and he began to study law under Thomas A. Ledwith, a young attorney who was a member of a prominent white family. Jim prepared legal papers, read law books, and assisted Mr. Ledwith. He studied in the early morning hours, in the afternoon until late at night, and on weekends and vacations.

Mr. Ledwith and Jim became good friends, and the student made rapid progress. At the end of eighteen months Mr. Ledwith thought Jim was ready to take the bar examination.

"Do you really think I could pass it?" Jim asked.

"Why not? You have been studying diligently. You have a good mind," Mr. Ledwith said.

"But I can't afford to make a mistake. There will be people who would be very happy if I failed," Jim said.

"Yes. Not everyone would like to see a black man become a a lawyer. But still, you are well known, and well liked."

"A Negro will need more than that," Jim said.

"Perhaps. But you've got it. I'm sure you will be able to pass the examination. If I were you, I would make my application."

"All right, if you say so. I only hope you are right."

Though he was doubtful, Jim made his application for admission to the bar. He knew that no Negro had been admitted to the Florida bar since Reconstruction days after the Civil War when a few black men had been appointed as lawyers. No Negro in Florida had ever passed an examination in law.

When he and Mr. Ledwith entered the courtroom, he was surprised to find it crowded. It was a large room, but never before had so many people been packed into it, not even for the most notorious murder trials.

Many people had come hoping to see a Negro fail. Others had come hoping to see him succeed. A number of lawyers of the county were present. It was important for Jim to succeed. Tension filled the room.

He knew the judge to be a just man, a good man as far as dealing with black people was concerned. A committee of three had been appointed to conduct the examination. One was a

leading member of the bar. Jim knew him also to be a fair and honorable man. Another was a young lawyer. The third was a man known by Negroes to be a "bad" white man, one without sympathy for or understanding of the black people.

Jim sat at the long table, facing the three examiners, with the judge on the bench in back of them. Nervously, his eyes moved toward the crowd that sat in the jury box at the side of the room. He caught the eye of Mr. Ledwith. His young teacher smiled and nodded his encouragement.

The examination started. The first question came. The silence in the room was deadly. Jim knew the answer. The second question came—and the answer. Jim felt easier. Then the questions came fast, one after the other. Jim answered promptly, but carefully. He did not allow himself to become excited. He considered each question and replied to it deliberately and as briefly as possible. He gained confidence. The examination was going very well.

When it seemed that the end should have been reached, the "bad" white lawyer opened the state statutes, and began to ask questions about them. Now, Jim was being examined in detail in many areas of law that were but little used and not well known even to experienced lawyers.

This was unfair. No lawyer can know all details of the many state statutes. Jim's heart sank. But he felt that the other lawyers in the room as well as the other members of the committee were shocked at the unfairness.

He resolved not to panic. He would stay with it and answer the questions as well as he could. He had studied hard and he had worked on Mr. Ledwith's cases and he had a much wider knowledge than even he thought. The questions went on and on.

Two hours later there was a pause. One of the lawyers whispered to the committee, "Don't you think this has gone on long enough?"

The most prominent member of the committee nodded. "I think so," he said. "Now what shall we do about it?"

Jim had clearly passed the examination. There was no doubt about how this last question should be answered.

There was a pause.

The "bad" man on the committee spoke up harshly. "Well, I don't care. I don't want to see any nigger made a member of this bar!" Fuming with anger he stalked out of the room.

Jim sat quietly while the committee conferred with the judge in whispers.

They returned to their seats. The judge asked Jim to stand. He did so, and solemnly took his oath as a lawyer.

He was a member of the Florida bar, the first Negro to be admitted upon examination.

10

A SONG IS BORN

ROSAMOND HAD SPENT six years in Boston studying music and had traveled with a musical play for a year. Two of his compositions had been published. He came back to Jacksonville to teach music.

"The theatrical bug has bitten me," he declared to his older brother.

"Is that serious?" Jim asked.

"I'm afraid it is. I wonder if it will bite you too. You'll catch it from me if you aren't careful, because I've got it bad."

"Not me. I'm a school principal and now I'm a lawyer too. You're the musician in the family," Jim said.

"You play a mean guitar. You can sing a song better than most. I tell you Jim, there's a lot that can be done with music."

"Not for me. I'm a word man. I feel better with pencil and paper than I do with music. I'll leave the music to you."

Rosamond opened a music studio in the Johnson home, and

soon had as many students as he could handle. The black community had never had a chance before to study music with a trained musician.

But Rosamond did get Jim interested in music. For the Stanton school graduation exercises the two young men prepared a special musical program. It was well received. Jim wrote the verses for some of Rosamond's music.

"You can write verses for more songs," said Rosamond.

"Well, maybe I'll work with you on another school program," Jim said.

"Look at this. I found some of your notebooks. They are filled with poems. I'm going to set some of them to music."

"Go ahead," said Jim.

"But what I really need is a book, a libretto, a story. Then I could write the music for an opera."

"An opera? That's for Verdi and Wagner and—"

"Well, call it a musical play if the word opera scares you."

Jim fell in with the idea and an opera began to take form. The words and the music came to life. They sang some of the songs at exercises at the school and at concerts that were given to show off the talents of Rosamond's students.

Their work became known in the musical circles in town and was much admired. A few prominent white people became interested and gave their encouragement. A party was arranged by one of the important white merchants at which Rosamond played and he and Jim sang the songs from their opera.

Jim became as interested in the musical play as Rosamond was.

"Don't laugh at me, Rozy, but I've got an idea," he said one day.

"It won't be the first idea you've had. What is it?" Rosamond asked.

"I think we ought to go to New York and try to sell this opera," Jim said bravely.

"Jim, you practically took the words out of my mouth," Rosamond replied. "I've been thinking about that too, but I didn't know what you would say."

"We'll be babes in the woods up there, but let's try it this summer after school closes."

"You've got a deal," said Rosamond.

When summer came, the two brothers set off for New York to sell their play. They took with them the good wishes of their hometown music lovers.

One of their white admirers in Florida gave them a letter of introduction which opened the way to a music publisher. But the musical play they had written, *Toloso*, was the best introduction. Several producers came to hear Jim and Rosamond play and sing it.

Soon they were meeting other show people. One was Bob Cole, a young Negro of great ability and experience in the theater. He could sing, dance, and act. He could direct, and had written a number of songs.

Jim, Rosamond, and Bob Cole wrote a song which they called
"Louisiana Lize." A well-known star, May Irwin, paid them
fifty dollars for the rights to sing it. A publisher agreed to pub-
lish it.

Then, suddenly the summer was gone. They did not sell their
opera, but they had met theatrical people and had discovered
enough of Broadway and the theater to want to see more of it.

"Gee, I'd like to stay here," said Rosamond.

"And I would too. But we can't live forever on May Irwin's
fifty dollars. Any royalties from the sheet music of "Louisiana
Lize" are still a dream. We've got to go back to our steady jobs,"
said Jim.

"I suppose so," Rosamond agreed sadly.

As the train sped back through the pine forests and the fields,
Rosamond and Jim were full of thoughts about another try at
Broadway.

That fall Jim wrote a poem which he called "Sence You
Went Away." He sent it to *Century* magazine, and it was accepted and published. It was a wonderful thrill to see his work
in print. He held up the small check in payment for the poem.
"I have the taste of writing in my mouth," he said happily.

"You have the taste of the theater in your mouth too. And
so have I," Rosamond said.

"Maybe," Jim agreed, as his mind went back to the exciting
summer in New York.

Rosamond set "Sence You Went Away" to music. It later

became a well-known song, sung by some of the best known singers.

Each song seemed to demand another. The Johnson brothers and some other young men planned a celebration for Lincoln's birthday. Jim wanted to write a poem about Lincoln. At first, the words did not readily fall into place. His pen was slow to move.

But finally a line did come. It would not go away. "Lift ev'ry voice and sing."

The line stayed with him. Other words came. This was different from his other poems. Suddenly words filled his mind. He was seized with a strange urgency he had never felt before.

He called Rosamond and recited the words. His brother sat at the piano, his hands moving over the keys.

Jim walked back and forth, caught up in the emotion of the creative moment that flooded through him. He had never felt anything so deeply, had never thought such excitement possible.

At last, he put the words down on paper.

> Lift ev'ry voice and sing
> Till earth and heaven ring,
> Ring with the harmonies of Liberty;
> Let our rejoicing rise
> High as the listening skies
> Let it resound loud as the rolling sea.
> Sing a song full of the faith that the dark past
>   has taught us.

Sing a song full of the hope that the present
    has brought us.
Facing the rising sun
Of our new day begun,
Let us march on till victory is won.

The song was sung at the Lincoln's birthday celebration. The children who performed it remembered it. Others who heard it sang it too. They took it with them wherever they went.

Later, the National Association for the Advancement of Colored People selected it as an official song. It would be known as the Negro National Hymn.

11

THERE'S NOTHING LIKE
SHOW BUSINESS

THE WINTER was a busy one. Jim's work at Stanton took most of his time. His small law practice made more demands, but he still found it possible to write a few poems and, with Rosamond, to create a song now and then.

"We'll go to New York again, won't we?" Jim asked.

"Bet your bottom dollar we will. Just as soon as summer comes," Rosamond replied.

"I'll be glad to see Bob Cole again."

"Me too. And good old Broadway too," Rosamond replied.

The summer of 1900 found them in New York. At once they formed a partnership with Bob Cole and soon they had written songs that were used by May Irwin in her new play.

Again there was the excitement of the theater and show business, and again the summer ended. Once more the two young

men returned to Jacksonville, with promises to Bob that they
would be back.

The summer's experience had been thrilling to them, but it
had also been costly. They were in debt and would have to
work all winter to pay the money they owed.

That winter Jim arranged for Paul Laurence Dunbar to come
to Jacksonville to read some of his poems. Dunbar was a well-
known Negro poet and his appearances were in great demand.
Jim had met him several years earlier and admired his work
greatly.

Negroes and whites crowded into the concert hall where Mr.
Dunbar appeared, as they had the year before when Rosamond
had arranged a concert for Sidney Woodward, a celebrated
Negro tenor from Boston. Jacksonville had never before had an
opportunity of hearing such talented gentlemen.

In the early summer of 1901, Jim and Rosamond were pre-
paring once again to go to New York. Their trip was delayed
by a fire which destroyed many buildings in town, including
Stanton school.

"But there is really nothing we can do here to help," Jim said.
"When we get to New York, perhaps we can arrange a benefit
to help some of the people whose homes have been destroyed."

"Good idea. Bob Cole will help us," said Rosamond.

"I'll write to him. We'll leave right away."

Bob was enthusiastic about the idea. The three young men
asked some of their Negro theatrical friends to help them. The
benefit performance earned almost a thousand dollars, which

Jim sent to the mayor of Jacksonville.

Once again Jim was in was in the center of the busy world of show business. He worked on a comic opera called *The Cannibal King* with Will Marion Cook, who was a successful musician of great talent.

News was received that Stanton could not be rebuilt until the middle of the winter. The Johnson brothers and Cole settled down to serious business. Music, songs, and shows appeared as if by magic. Music for *Champagne Charlie*. Specialty numbers for *The Sleeping Beauty*. A musical comedy called *The Supper Club*. Some of their melodies brought them quick fame: "Tell Me, Dusky Maiden," "Nobody's Lookin' but the Owl and the Moon," and "Come Out, Dinah, on the Green."

One of their songs, "The Maiden with the Dreamy Eyes," was sung by the great singing star, Anna Held. A child star named Elsie Janis helped bring it to popularity.

Florenz Ziegfeld and other famous producers sought them out. The three artists were in the center of the Broadway musical theater. The great stars, black and white, were their friends.

Late in the summer they delivered fifteen songs to their publisher, Jos. W. Stern and Co. But it was a long time between signing a publishing contract and the receipt of royalties which were to be paid every six months. In February, Stanton was to be finished. Jim felt he ought to go back to his steady job.

"That settles it for me. I've got to go back to school books and briefs," said Jim.

"I'm not going back," said Rosamond. "Bob and I will work up a vaudeville act. I know we can get some bookings."

"Fellows, will you lend me some money so I can get back to Florida?" Jim asked.

"Sure," said Rosamond. "And we'll see you next summer."

"I don't know. Not unless some royalty checks come. A steady job means a lot," Jim said.

He was very disappointed when he got back to Jacksonville and saw the new Stanton school that had been built after the fire. "What an awful looking building," he said. "How could they build such a thing? It looks like a warehouse."

"I've heard that the school board intends it to be only a temporary building," his father said.

"Why?"

"I don't know. I can only tell you what I've heard."

It didn't seem reasonable to Jim. The location was a good one, an excellent one. He talked with some of his lawyer friends. When he spoke to men on the school board, he tried to find out what was going on, why an attractive, permanent building had not been erected.

Gradually the story came to light. The land had become "too valuable." Certain interests in town had come to think that the Negro school should be in a less convenient location and that the Stanton plot should be sold.

Stanton had long been an important part of the Negro community. It was a source of pride to the black people. Jim was

dismayed and shocked. He would have to do something. But what?

As he thought about it, he seemed to remember he had heard that Stanton had been given to the community as a school for black people. He didn't know the facts. He only had a dim recollection.

"What am I doing?" he said to himself. "There is a way to find out. I'm a lawyer. I'll go to the courthouse and look up the records."

Early the next day he was in the back room of the courthouse where the old records were kept. Quickly he searched through the dusty volumes. Ah, here was something.

It was a deed from Governor Hart, who had been governor of Florida during Reconstruction days, to a board of trustees of black men and white men. It was not a deed to the city, nor to the county, or the state, or the board of education. It was to trustees, and they were bound by its terms.

And the terms? His eyes followed the lines of the old script. The plot should be used only for the purpose of a Negro school. And if it was ever not needed for that purpose and if it was ever used for any other purpose, the land would revert to the heirs of Governor Hart!

The trustees had grown old or had died, but the trust remained. The school board had changed and everyone had forgotten about the deed. It was a happy day when Jim was able to report the facts of the trust to the school board.

Stanton was saved.

12

TO THE TOP

Deep down Jim had wanted to stay in New York. But what would the future of Stanton have been if he had not made his search of the old records? Broadway was more fun, but perhaps teaching was more important. He pushed his summer experiences out of his mind and settled down to the serious work of teacher and school principal.

The year before he had been elected president of the State Teachers' Association. He began studying for the examination for a lifetime teaching certificate.

Rosamond and Bob kept in touch. They had met with some success and had a few bookings for their vaudeville act.

One day, shortly after school had closed for the summer, Jim was hard at work studying when a letter arrived from Rosamond. Eager for news, he tore open the envelope and began to read. The songs they had written were beginning to sell.

They were out of debt, and there was money left over. Money orders for $480 fell from the envelope.

Jim sprang to his feet. All thought of study left him. He ran to his mother. Dancing around her, he showered the pages of the letter and the money orders into her lap.

"I'm going to New York!" he cried. "I'm going to New York! Rozy says our songs are selling well. I want to write more of them."

"New York? But your teaching? Stanton?"

"They aren't for me. Not now," Jim exclaimed joyfully.

There was another reason Jim wanted to return North. Resentment and prejudice against Negroes were particularly bad in Jacksonville. Jim himself had felt it personally in an incident after the big fire. A woman journalist from New York had written an article about the disaster and asked Jim to read it over before she submitted it to newspapers. He agreed, and met her in the park to go over the material. Walking back, they were overtaken by angry militiamen with bloodhounds. Jim was arrested. A Negro man was walking with a white woman in the park! That wasn't allowed in Florida.

There were some frightening moments before things were straightened out. The fair-skinned woman was actually a Negro too. But the hatred shown toward Jim, who had many friends both white and black, was hard to forget or forgive.

Back with Rosamond and Bob Cole, Jim was swept into a whirl of activity. The fever of the musical and theatrical world

took hold. The three worked hard, turning out songs and plays. The future for Bob Cole and the Johnson brothers looked promising.

As the weeks wore on, Jim realized that a decision had to be made. Should he stay in the uncertain world of show business or return to Stanton? Would the songs really be a success? Would they continue to sell?

He wrote a letter of resignation to the school, but did not mail it. One evening as he was taking a walk with Bob and Rosamond, he paused in front of a mailbox. He held the letter in his hand. "Shall I mail it?" he asked.

"It's a tough decision," said Rosamond.

The letter hovered above the gaping mail slot, then Jim dropped it. "I'll send it," he declared. "I know we can succeed with our music." The ties with Stanton were cut.

Jim was right. They did succeed. They reached peaks they never dreamed possible. The name, Cole and Johnson Brothers, appeared more and more often on the covers of sheet music, in theatrical programs, in the papers, and on the tongues of the great and small people in show business. Songs such as "Under the Bamboo Tree," "The Congo Love Song," "Fishing," and many more tunes were sung by stars and by an eager public. The popular composers worked for Klaw and Erlanger, the leading producers. They had a good contract with their publishers. Famous people were their friends.

With Rosamond and Bob away on the road with their vaudeville act so much, Jim decided to enroll at Columbia University for courses in English, history, and drama. The desire to write was always with him, and the professors were most encouraging. He started a novel, to be called *The Autobiography of an Ex-Colored Man*, about a light-skinned Negro who "passed" as a white man. When it was later published it caused quite a stir. He also continued writing poems, many of which appeared in magazines.

When the team of Bob Cole and Rosamond Johnson was booked for a tour across the country, Jim went with them. They were smash hits. Where they went, what they did was news. But that did not prevent them from meeting the same prejudice that other Negroes had to put up with. There were hotels that did not have rooms for them, restaurants where they were not welcome, barbers who would not cut their hair. Even in theaters where they were appearing, the best seats were not sold to Negroes. It was wrong. Jim wondered if his mother was right when she told him that such wrongs would be righted some day.

Then the Cole-Johnson team had a chance to take their act to London. Jim and Bob and Rosamond made the trip a tour of Europe as well. They had a marvelous time. London gave them a warm welcome. It was great to be at the top.

13

THE CONSUL

In 1904, Theodore Roosevelt was running for President. Charles W. Anderson, a prominent Negro politician in New York whom Jim had known for some years, asked him to help establish a Republican political club. Jim agreed, and talked Bob Cole and Rosamond into helping write the campaign song for Teddy Roosevelt.

Roosevelt won the election, and Charles Anderson was appointed Collector of Internal Revenue for New York City. Jim became president of the political club.

One day Mr. Anderson suggested that Jim go into the Consular Service, representing his government abroad. "With your ability to speak Spanish so well, you could do a good job, especially in South American countries," he said.

Jim said he would think it over. The idea appealed to him. In the spring he passed the necessary examination and was appointed United States Consul at Puerto Cabello in Venezuela. His work in show business had been exciting, but there was more serious writing he wanted to do. Though he would be the guardian and protector of the interests of the United States in Venezuela, there would be time for thinking and creating. There, he completed the novel he had started at Columbia. He also wrote more poetry.

In 1909, he was promoted and sent to Corinto, a port city in Nicaragua. There, the quiet diplomatic life came to an end when a revolution broke out. As Consul, the safety of United States citizens and their property was in Jim's hands.

Rebel forces were trying to overthrow the dictator of Nicaragua, and most of the fighting went on in the interior of the country. But the revolutionists threatened to take over the port of Corinto, and the local Commandante looked to the Americans for help in opposing them. The United States Consul was on the spot.

There was an American warship in the harbor, but most of its crew had been sent inland to the capital. Only fourteen armed sailors were left in the town for protection of the consulate and the many people who had taken refuge there. The U.S.S. *Denver* with reinforcements was expected any moment. What delayed her, no one knew.

Representatives from the rebels demanded that the city be turned over to them. In order to stall for time until the *Denver* could arrive, Consul Johnson allowed them to come into town for a conference with him. They were housed a few blocks from the consulate.

In the evening they were to be escorted to the conference, and it was decided to make the most of the small force of four-teen sailors. Each one, stationed at intervals along the way, challenged the party with a firm "Halt! Who goes there?" Only when the escort identified himself did they allow them to pass. With so many sentries, the rebels naturally thought there were hundreds of troops.

At the meeting the rebel leaders repeated their demands to hand over the port, and threatened to take it with 3,000 troops. Jim talked with them patiently, but it was obvious that they did not want to be reasonable. So he invited them to dine with him.

Earlier he had ordered a huge roast beef dinner to be pre-pared, with no limits on the alcoholic beverages. The rebels were delighted. They ate heartily and drank even more heartily. Before long they forgot their angry demands. The American Consul was a wonderful host. A real prince! A great man! Soon sleep became more important than the revolution.

Jim ordered them put aboard the train and taken back to their headquarters inland. He was dead tired. And where was the *Denver*? Without the marines it was bringing, he could do nothing.

The next day the rebel representatives sent a message de-manding another conference. Consul Johnson feared that if he let them come back into the city, fighting would break out, so

he met them at a pass in the mountains. "We demand that you turn the port of Corinto over to us," they said.

Jim had to play for more time. to give the *Denver* with her marines a chance to reach the harbor. "You must give me an official paper from your general showing that you have the power to act for him," he said.

"We will have the paper for you tomorrow."

Tomorrow. That would give him a full day's delay. "Very well. I will wait for it," he said.

It was dark when he got back to the consulate. Though he was very tired, his sleep was restless. The safety of the city was at stake.

He was up with the sun. A deep fog covered the bay. As he watched, the mist cleared and he saw a ship coming toward land. It was a United States Navy ship. It was the U.S.S. *Denver*!

Five hundred marines were landed and Corinto was safe. That night Consul James Weldon Johnson slept soundly for the first time in many nights.

14

ROMANCE FOR A
DIPLOMAT

WHEN JIM GOT leave while in Corinto, he returned to Washington and New York and saw Rosamond and Bob. He also saw someone else—a Miss Grace Nail, whom he had met earlier while he was in New York writing songs. She was a beautiful, artistic, and well-educated young woman, and he always enjoyed her company. He asked her to be his wife, and in 1910 they were married.

Jim brought his bride to Corinto. Grace was fascinated with the Latin-American cities they visited on the way, and quickly learned Spanish. She made a gracious hostess for the consulate. Fortunately, the couple had been on leave just before the revolution broke out and she remained in New York during that tense period.

After so long a time in the tropics, Jim applied for a new post. He hoped for a position in France, but was listed for the Azores. That would be next best, but even that was not to be. A change in political administrations left no hope of anything more than perhaps another tour of duty in Corinto. He did not want that, and sent in his resignation.

Jim and Grace went to Jacksonville for a while. Jim's father had passed away, but his mother was there, and there were business matters to be settled.

Jim did not want to remain in Jacksonville. He could do more in New York. He wanted to write. He wanted to help his people. Wherever he went, he still met the resentment toward colored people that he had lived with all his life. There must be something he could do about it.

The Johnsons went to live in New York. Jim wondered if he could make a living with his writing. Then a bit of good fortune came at just the right time. He was asked to be the editor of *The New York Age*, a Negro newspaper. Now he could present his ideas and there would be an audience to read his words.

Jim agreed to write the editorials for *The New York Age* and did so for ten years. Meanwhile, he did other writing—poems, songs, articles. With Victor Herbert, the well-known composer, and others he helped organize ASCAP, the American Society of Composers, Authors, and Publishers, designed to protect musicians by regulating the collection of royalties. He translated into English the Spanish opera, *Goyescas*, and saw it produced at the Metropolitan Opera House in New York in 1915.

One day a letter came from J. E. Spingarn, asking Jim to participate in a conference sponsored by the National Association for the Advancement of Colored People. Spingarn was chairman of the board of the association, and W.E.B. Du Bois, the prominent Negro leader whom Jim had met as a young man, was active in it. The organization was set up to promote the rights of Negroes.

James Weldon Johnson did participate in the conference. Later that year he was invited to be a field secretary for the NAACP.

"It's like the hand of destiny," he told Grace. "All these years I have wanted to turn my energies to helping black people. Now I will have a real opportunity."

Remembering all the injustices Negroes suffered, Jim took advantage of that opportunity. He set to work organizing new branches of the association, investigating riots, promoting efforts to obtain equal voting rights. The Association grew rapidly. Throughout all his work for the NAACP, Jim firmly believed that the task of improving the lot of Negroes would rest with the Negro himself. Education was the key.

When the United States entered World War I in 1917, black men were drafted and volunteered for the army, but there was no chance for Negroes to become officers. Jim and a committee

from the NAACP brought the facts before the Secretary of War.

"No one can question the loyalty of black citizens," Jim pointed out. "The country is concerned about the possibility of spies and betrayal. And all the guards at the White House and at the State, Army, and Navy buildings are black men."

The arguments were persuasive. A special training camp for Negro officers was set up at Des Moines, Iowa. Over 600 colored men received commissions in the Army.

A race riot in East St. Louis occurred in the summer of 1917. Jim and others in the NAACP were shocked. They wanted to protest such happenings, and Jim suggested a silent protest parade down Fifth Avenue in New York City.

The country had seen nothing like it. Ten thousand Negroes —little children, women, men—marched silently down the street. Only muffled drums accompanied them. The people lining the sidewalks to watch stood in silence. It was strangely moving, and most impressive.

15

A LIFE WELL SPENT

JAMES WELDON JOHNSON continued his work with the NAACP. He was named Secretary in 1920, the first Negro to hold that position. There was so much to be done. He wanted to accomplish what he could. He made speeches, he attended conferences, the President sought his advice. Whatever concerned the Negro concerned him.

But despite his long hours devoted to the cause of his race, he found time to collect his poems into a volume entitled *Fifty Years and Other Poems*. The title poem had been written in celebration of the fiftieth anniversary of the Emancipation Proclamation. Later, other books appeared—an anthology of American Negro poetry, two volumes of Negro spirituals, *God's Trombones* which was seven Negro sermons in verse, *Black Manhattan*, and another collection of poems entitled *St. Peter Relates an Incident of the Resurrection Day*.

His brother Rosamond made piano arrangements for the two books of Negro spirituals. Rosamond had married while he was in London as supervisor of music at the Opera House there. He had returned to New York to become director of the New York Music School Settlement for Colored People.

Honors came to James Weldon Johnson. He was awarded the Spingarn Medal for "the highest or noblest achievement by an American Negro." He won the Harmon Award for his book of poetry, *God's Trombones*. He was elected to the board of trustees of Atlanta University. The Julius Rosenwald Fund offered him a fellowship which enabled him to devote his time to writing for a year.

Throughout it all he kept up his activities in behalf of colored people. He fought for enactment of an antilynching bill. Organizations wanted his help, and he gave it to the National Interracial Conference, the Institute of Pacific Relations, the Civil Liberties Union, and many others. He was intent on making America better for black people, and in making black people better for America.

James Weldon Johnson was offered the Adam K. Spence Chair of Creative Literature at Fisk University, and he gladly accepted. "I started out as a teacher," he told his wife. "I like to think that I inspired some of my high school students. Perhaps I can do the same as a university professor." He also became a lecturer in Negro history and art at New York University. *Along This Way*, Jim's autobiography, appeared in 1933. *Negro*

Americans, What Now? followed in 1934.

For some years the Johnsons had a summer place called "Five Acres" at Great Barrington, Massachusetts. On June 26, 1938, when he was on a vacation in Maine, James Weldon Johnson's automobile was struck at a railway crossing and he was killed. It was a sad day for his nation. Great figures and little people mourned his passing. Hundreds attended his funeral in Harlem.

James Weldon Johnson was a teacher, lawyer, editor, poet, songwriter, diplomat, politician, social and civil rights advocate, a crusader for democracy. He knew that black people had done a great deal for America and had played an important part in its development. He argued that they deserved greater recognition and increased opportunity. He cried out against poverty, discrimination, and oppression. With clarity and logic, he fought for equality for his people and for all people.

Always he encouraged his own people to do the best they could. "Lift ev'ry voice and sing . . . Sing a song full of the faith that the dark past has taught us. Sing a song full of the hope that the present has brought us . . ."

LIFT EV'RY VOICE AND SING

Piano and guitar arrangement by
Edward V. Bonnemère

Music and lyrics by James Weldon Johnson
and J. Rosamond Johnson

Copyright MCMXXI by Edward B. Marks Music Corporation
Copyright renewed MCMXLIX by Edward B. Marks Music Corporation
© Copyright MCMLXXI by Edward B. Marks Music Corporation
Used by permission

| | Bb | F° | D° | F | | C#° | Dm | C7 | | F | |

skies, Let it re - sound loud as the roll — ing sea.
feet, Come to the place for which our fa - thers sighed?
light, Keep us for - ev - er in the path,— we pray.

pp *poco meno mosso*   F   F6

Sing   a   song   full   of   the   faith that the dark past has
We   have   come   o - ver   a   way that with tears has been
Lest   our   feet   stray from the   pla - ces, our God, where we

pp *poco meno mosso*

F   F   Db   *rall. e molto cresc.*

taught   us;   Sing   a   song   full   of   the
wa - tered;   We   have   come,   tread - ing   our
met   Thee,   Lest   our   hearts, drunk with the

sfz   *rall. e molto cresc.*

THE AUTHOR

HAROLD W. FELTON, a lawyer by profession, is an author known for his tall tales and his biographies for young readers. A long-time interest in American folklore led to the first of his widely acclaimed books, an anthology of legends about Paul Bunyan. Since that time he has pursued folk heroes with enthusiasm, and his stories about Pecos Bill, John Henry, Fire-Fightin' Mose, Bowleg Bill, and Sergeant O'Keefe rank him as a master yarn spinner.

In A HORSE NAMED JUSTIN MORGAN, Mr. Felton dealt with facts that seemed like tall tales—history that was "almost too good to be true." Turning to the lives of Jim Beckwourth, Edward Rose, and Nat Love, he discovered the same sort of material—biographies more astonishing than fiction.

Long a resident of New York City, Mr. Felton and his wife now reside in Falls Village, Connecticut. His most recent book was MUMBET: The Story of Elizabeth Freeman.

THE ILLUSTRATOR

CHARLES SHAW lives in Austin, Texas, where he is currently art director for *Texas Parks and Wildlife* magazine. His work has appeared in books and periodicals, and his pen-and-ink drawings are part of the Air Force Historical Art Collection. He is a member of the New York Society of Illustrators, and has won awards in Austin, Amarillo, Houston, and Denver.

LIBRARY
ANDERSON ELEMENTARY SCHOOL

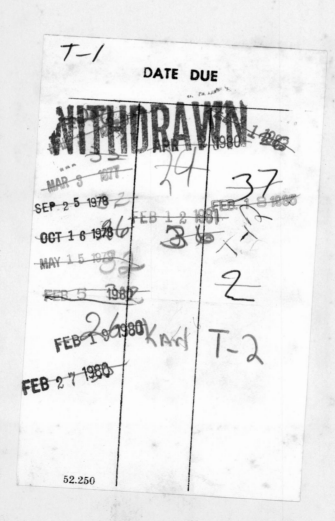

T-1

DATE DUE

WITHDRAWN

MAR 3 1977

SEP 2 5 1978

OCT 1 6 1978

MAY 1 5 1979

FEB 5 1980

FEB 1 9 1980

FEB 2 7 1980

FEB 1 2 1981

FEB 1 8 1985

T-2

52.250